TRANSPORT NETWORKS

Jack and Meg Gillett

With contributions by Richard and Louise Spilsbury

WAYLAND

Contents

About this book

Transport is the movement of goods or people between places. It almost always involves vehicles, ranging from trains to aircraft. But transport can also mean pumping materials, such as gas and oil, through pipes. Transport networks are interconnected routes and types of transport that regularly operate across specific areas. These areas can be local, regional, national and even global in scale.

This book looks at some of the different types of transport that exist around the world. These vary, depending on their use. For example, transport and transport networks that office workers use to commute into cities are very different from those used to move heavy goods between countries. The shape and scale of transport networks in any country are strongly influenced by its geographical setting, for example landscape features and climate. A country may also arrange some of its transport networks according to where it has natural resources and where they are in demand.

Transport and transport networks are vital to the industry and economy of an area. They are used to distribute goods and resources, supply energy and connect people. However, there are also environmental impacts from building and using transport networks, which include pollution, the destruction of natural habitats and contributing to global warming.

Map shows the transport networks discussed

Globe shows the location of the map region

Fun research activity

Key explains the symbols used in the map

Statistical feature for at-a-glance data

Pictures highlight features discussed or located on the map

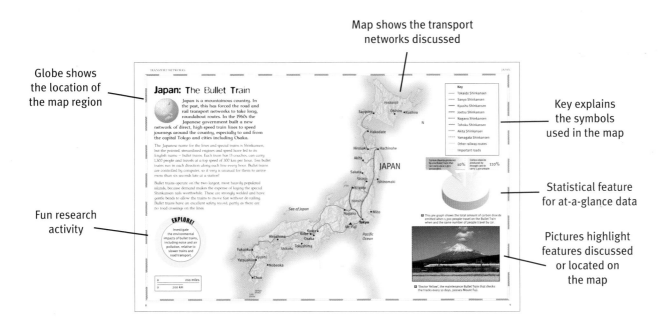

Prague: Commuting by tram

Prague is the busy capital city of the Czech Republic in central Europe. Around 1.2 million people live in Prague, which covers nearly 500 km². Most of Prague's residents rely on public transport to move from large housing areas on the outskirts, many with high-rise apartments, to work or study in the old city centre.

The centre of Prague was rebuilt in the 18th century after a destructive fire. The buildings are close together and the streets mostly narrow because the main transport then was horse-drawn carriages. When the city grew during the Industrial Revolution, new buildings spread outwards from the centre to house its growing population. The city layout that developed affected how the tram network expanded, too.

Trams are an ideal urban transport for Prague and many other tight city centres. Compared to buses, they can carry more people, they don't cause congestion and they create far less air pollution because they are electric. As the rails run along existing roads, using the same road network, tram lines do not disrupt the traffic or need extra space through the buildings of the city.

Prague's tram network is one of the biggest in Europe. It has 141 km of track and 37 different lines, although only the busiest ones are shown on the map. There are 1000 tram cars carrying around 300 million people a year. Globally, trams will become more popular in the future as more governments look to provide urban transport with low environmental impact.

20 26

1 2 18

8 22

7 9 10

B
park & ride

← Bigger and better trams are gradually replacing older models such as this Tatra T3 to cope with the growing population in Prague.

Topological map of Prague's tram and metro routes

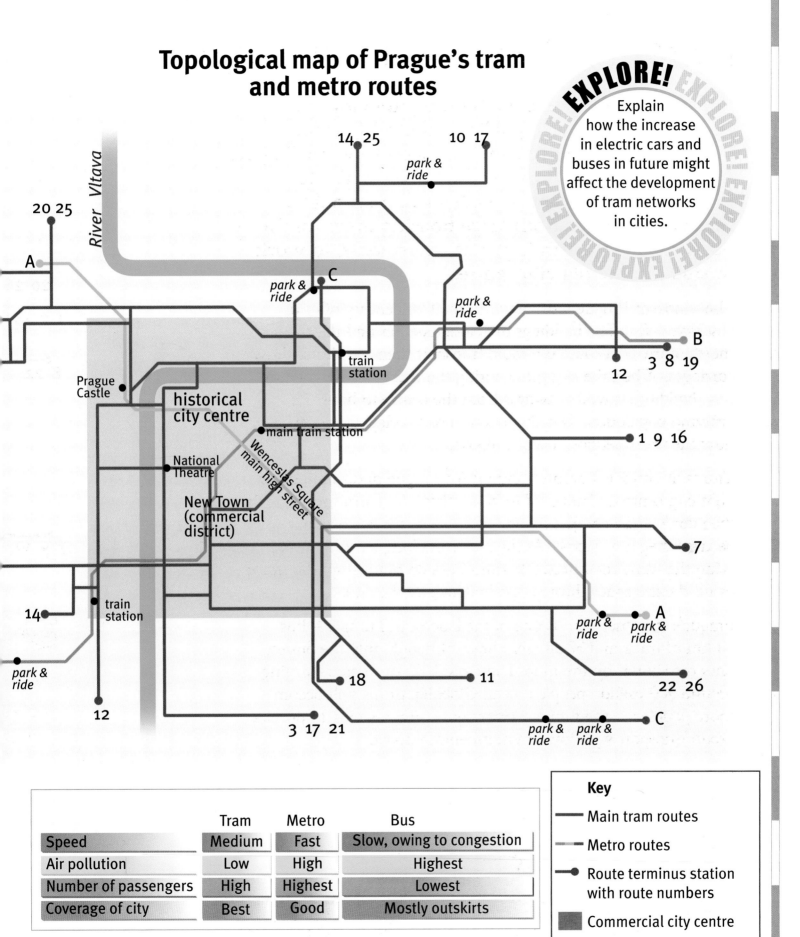

EXPLORE!

Explain how the increase in electric cars and buses in future might affect the development of tram networks in cities.

	Tram	Metro	Bus
Speed	Medium	Fast	Slow, owing to congestion
Air pollution	Low	High	Highest
Number of passengers	High	Highest	Lowest
Coverage of city	Best	Good	Mostly outskirts

⬆ This table compares the most common forms of inner-city transport and transport networks.

Key

— Main tram routes

— Metro routes

●— Route terminus station with route numbers

▮ Commercial city centre

▮ Residential area

San Francisco Bay Area:
The B.A.R.T. network

The San Francisco Bay Area in California, USA, includes San Francisco and cities around the San Francisco and San Pablo bays. The Bay Area is home to nearly 8 million people, many of whom commute into cities.

In the 1970s, commuters faced long car journeys owing to congestion, bridge closures around the bays and also hazardous smog from the vehicle fumes. In 1978, the Bay Area Rapid Transit (B.A.R.T.) train network of rail lines and tunnels under the bays was built to improve commuting.

Today, trains carry over one third of a million commuters to work each day, in just a quarter of the driving time. All five routes on the network have been built to withstand earthquakes, caused by movements of the fault line under California. For example, B.A.R.T. lines were unaffected by the 1989 earthquake, whereas road bridges collapsed.

Using B.A.R.T. saves money on fuel, parking and road tolls, and lowers environmental impact, especially as the trains use mostly electricity from hydropower plants. However, many people still commute by car in the Bay Area, although car-sharing is an increasingly popular transport option.

EXPLORE!

Find out how much greenhouse gas is saved per person on a train commute compared to one in a car and work out the annual greenhouse gas reduction due to B.A.R.T..

⬆ A B.A.R.T. train at Daly City station.

B.A.R.T. statistics

Cost of network in 2004	$1.6 billion
Total length of track	167 km
Number of stations	43
Total number of carriages	670
Maximum train speed	120 km per hour
Train control	By computer – driver takes over in an emergency
Train frequency	Every 1 ½ minutes during the day Every 20 minutes at night
Passengers carried daily	350,000

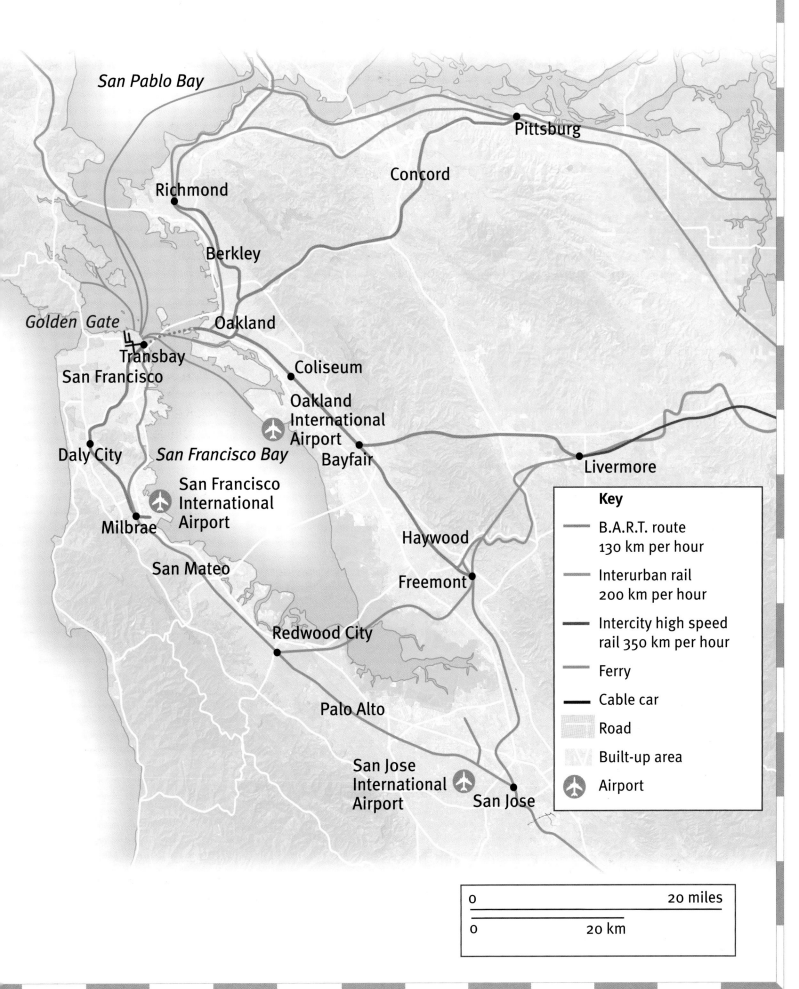

San Pablo Bay

Pittsburg

Concord

Richmond

Berkley

Golden Gate

Oakland

Transbay

San Francisco

Coliseum

Oakland International Airport

Bayfair

Daly City

San Francisco Bay

San Francisco International Airport

Milbrae

San Mateo

Livermore

Haywood

Freemont

Redwood City

Palo Alto

San Jose International Airport

San Jose

Key

———	B.A.R.T. route 130 km per hour
———	Interurban rail 200 km per hour
———	Intercity high speed rail 350 km per hour
———	Ferry
———	Cable car
▦	Road
▨	Built-up area
✈	Airport

0		20 miles
0	20 km	

Japan: The Bullet Train

Japan is a mountainous country. In the past, this has forced the road and rail transport networks to take long, roundabout routes. In the 1960s the Japanese government built a new network of direct, high-speed train lines to speed journeys around the country, especially to and from the capital Tokyo and cities including Osaka.

The Japanese name for the lines and special trains is Shinkansen, but the pointed, streamlined engines and speed have led to its English name — bullet trains. Each train has 13 coaches, can carry 1,300 people and travels at a top speed of 300 km per hour. Ten bullet trains run in each direction along each line every hour. Bullet trains are controlled by computer, so it very is unusual for them to arrive more than six seconds late at a station!

Bullet trains operate on the two largest, most heavily populated islands, because demand makes the expense of laying the special Shinkansen rails worthwhile. These are strongly welded and have gentle bends to allow the trains to move fast without de-railing. Bullet trains have an excellent safety record, partly as there are no road crossings on the lines.

EXPLORE!

Investigate the environmental impacts of bullet trains, including noise and air pollution, relative to slower trains and road transport.

0	200 miles
0	200 km

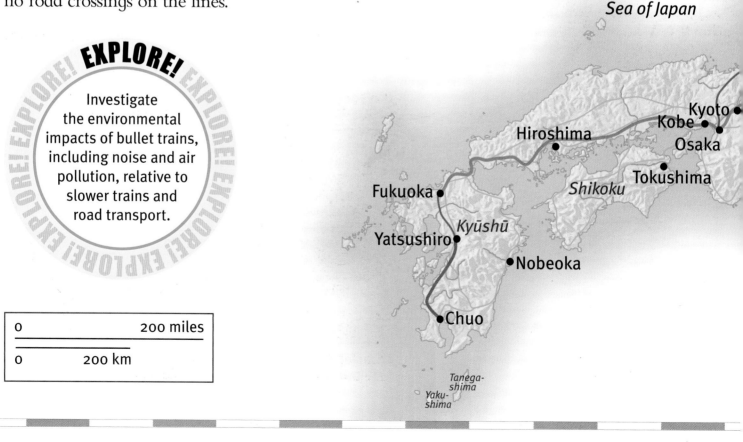

Sea of Japan

Kyoto

Kobe

Osaka

Hiroshima

Tokushima

Shikoku

Fukuoka

Kyūshū

Yatsushiro

Nobeoka

Chuo

Tanega-shima

Yaku-shima

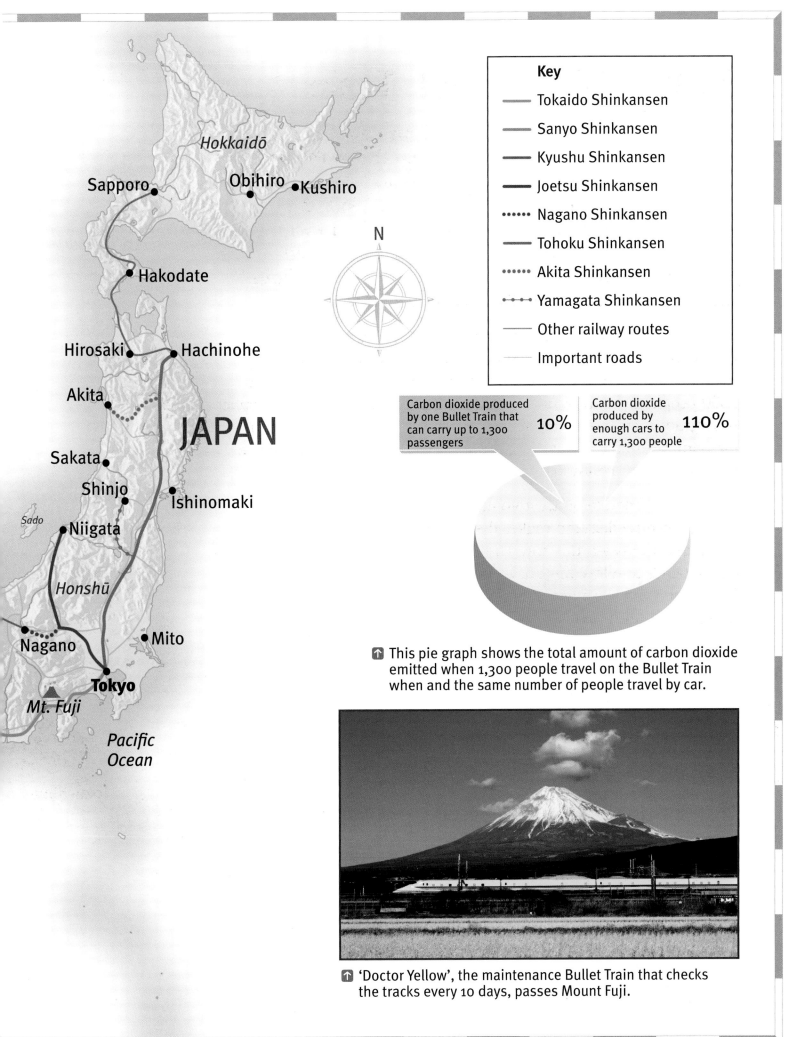

Key

———	Tokaido Shinkansen
———	Sanyo Shinkansen
———	Kyushu Shinkansen
———	Joetsu Shinkansen
••••••	Nagano Shinkansen
———	Tohoku Shinkansen
••••••	Akita Shinkansen
••••	Yamagata Shinkansen
———	Other railway routes
———	Important roads

Carbon dioxide produced by one Bullet Train that can carry up to 1,300 passengers **10%**

Carbon dioxide produced by enough cars to carry 1,300 people **110%**

⬆ This pie graph shows the total amount of carbon dioxide emitted when 1,300 people travel on the Bullet Train when and the same number of people travel by car.

⬆ 'Doctor Yellow', the maintenance Bullet Train that checks the tracks every 10 days, passes Mount Fuji.

9

Australia: Tourism by train

The first European settlers in Australia in the 18th century lived in coastal colonies. But they soon moved inland to find farmland and areas for gold mining. Overland transport of people and goods by foot or wagon was difficult over the hot, dry and rugged land.

Transcontinental lines were built from the early 20th century to improve trade. For example, the Ghan route (named after Afghan camels that used to carry goods on this route) links Darwin – a major port trading with Asia – with Adelaide and other large cities in the south of the country. The transcontinental rail network took decades to build owing to expense and problems including flooded land and termites eating wooden railway sleepers!

Today, transcontinental trains are a major draw for tourists. Rail transport across the country in air-conditioned carriages is more comfortable than in cars or buses and allows better sight-seeing than aircraft. Although the network accesses big tourist attractions such as Uluru, it does not cover some parts of the country with few settlements, so tourists still need to use other forms of transport to see those areas.

Indian Ocean

•Broome

Great Sandy Desert

•
Dampier

Karijini *National Park*

Little Sandy Desert

WESTERN AUSTRALIA

Kalbarri *National Park*

Gold mines of Kalgoorie

Kalgoorie •

Perth •
• Fremantle

The Indian-Pacific Line is Australia's longest railway. It takes three nights and two full days to complete the journey between Perth and Sydney. One of its stops is at Australia's smallest town, called Cook, which has a total population of only two people!

N

Coral Sea

Uluru is one of Australia's most popular tourist attractions and Ghan Line passengers can visit it by coach from Alice Springs railway station. It is the most sacred natural place to Aborigines.

Key

—— The Ghan
—— The Indian Pacific
—— The Inlander
—— Spirit of the Outback
—— The Westlander
[📷] Tourist attraction
[✈] Airport

Darwin
Kakadu National Park

Great Barrier Reef

Cairns [✈]

NORTHERN TERRITORY

Townsville

Tanami Desert

Mount Isa

AUSTRALIA

Alice Springs

▲ Uluru (Ayers Rock)

Simpson Desert Conservation Park

QUEENSLAND

Longreach
Rockhampton

Charleville

SOUTH AUSTRALIA

Brisbane [✈]

Lake Eyre North
Lake Eyre National Park

Coober Pedy
Coober Pedy opal mines
Tarcoola

NEW SOUTH WALES

Great Victoria Desert

Lake Torrens

Lake Gairdner

Barossa Valley vinyards

Port Augusta

Blue Mountains National Park [✈]

Newcastle
Sydney

[✈] Adelaide

Canberra

VICTORIA

[✈]

Melbourne [✈]

Southern Ocean

0	500 miles
0	500 km

Tasmania

[✈]

Hobart

EXPLORE!

Research the trains used on transcontinental Australian railways and road trains. How much cargo can they carry and how do they compare in environmental impact?

Italy: Motorway links

Italy is a highly industrialised European country with well-developed road and rail networks. It was the first country in the world to build motorways, known as Autostrada, in the 1920s, to improve transport between the regions.

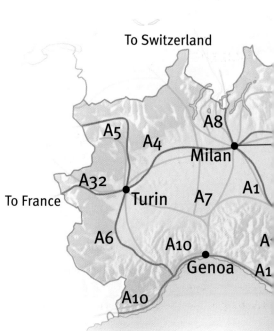

The Auto del Sol was built in the 1950s and 60s to make the Mezzogiorno region in the south more attractive to tourists, to help southern farmers sell their produce, such as olive oil and grapes, in the richer north and to prevent migration of southerners to work in northern industries.

Motorways have advantages over other roads. Traffic can move fast as there are no traffic lights, road junctions, or oncoming traffic on the same carriageway. Drivers have emergency lanes and telephones to access help when in difficulty and regular service stations for rest, food and fuel stops. However, the volume of traffic on motorways causes environmental problems including air and noise pollution. Building motorways can destroy habitats for wildlife and also bypass towns affecting trade and tourism.

Italian motorways are especially congested in the north, owing to the number of people living there and the transport links with the rest of Europe. The Frejus road tunnel on the A32 motorway near Turin carries around 80 per cent of freight traffic between Italy and France. This route is becoming so slow that Italy is building a newer, bigger rail tunnel nearby by 2020 to transport more of the freight.

Key

Mezzogiorno region

—— Motorways

—— Train lines

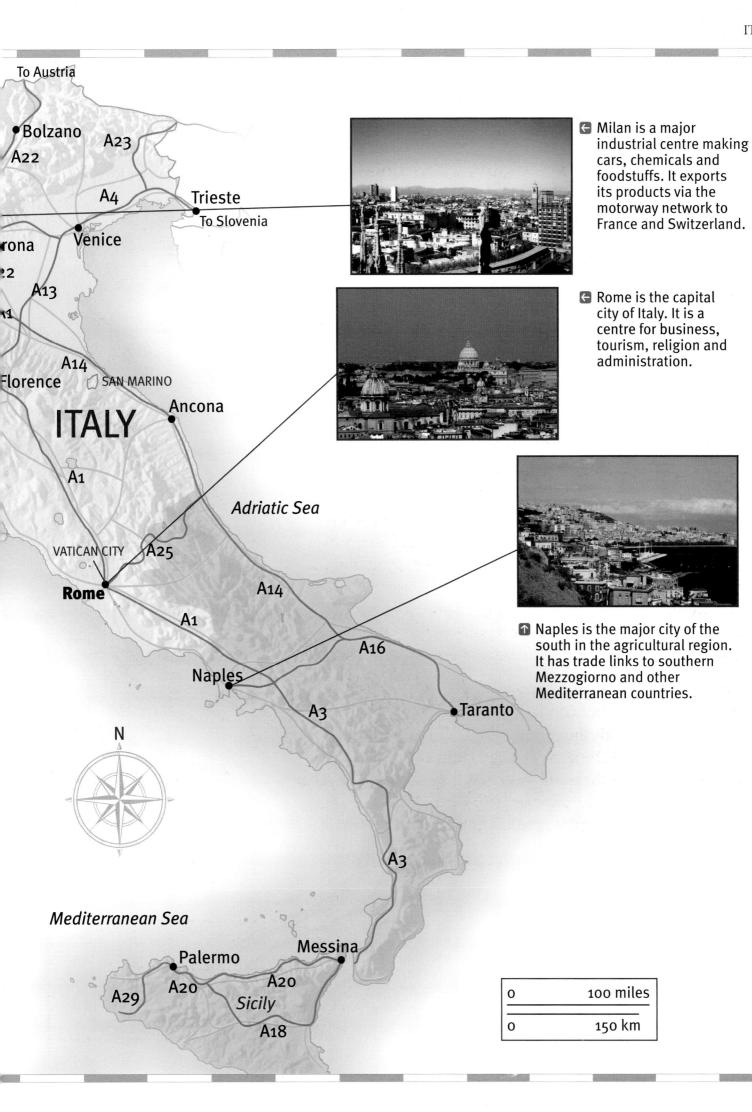

To Austria

Bolzano

A22

A23

A4

Trieste

To Slovenia

Venice

rona

22

A13

1

A14

Florence

SAN MARINO

Ancona

ITALY

A1

Adriatic Sea

VATICAN CITY

A25

Rome

A14

A1

Naples

A16

A3

Taranto

N

A3

Mediterranean Sea

Messina

Palermo

A20

A20

A29

Sicily

A18

← Milan is a major industrial centre making cars, chemicals and foodstuffs. It exports its products via the motorway network to France and Switzerland.

← Rome is the capital city of Italy. It is a centre for business, tourism, religion and administration.

↑ Naples is the major city of the south in the agricultural region. It has trade links to southern Mezzogiorno and other Mediterranean countries.

0	100 miles
0	150 km

Brazil: Transport expansion

Brazil has half of South America's total land area and population, its biggest city (São Paulo), as well as its largest rainforest. As Brazil continues to built its economy, it is expanding its transport networks from the coastal cities into the interior and linking with other parts of South America.

Economic development of a country usually happens by increasing the industry output or the range of industries, so people can make more money and improve their lives. Industrial development and access to goods relies on good transport networks. In Brazil, better transport enables the movement and sale or use of materials, ranging from forest timber and iron ore to beef for export and ethanol for vehicle fuel.

To support Brazil's economy, the government laid roads across this vast country and encouraged foreign companies to set up car factories and cattle ranches there. Expanding agriculture has lead to large-scale deforestation, and building the roads devastated large parts of the Amazon rainforest, but also allowed better access to other people. These included hunters, farmers and miners who have cleared more land and endangered wildlife and the cultures of native peoples.

COLOMBIA

R. Amazon

R. Juruá

Cruzeiro do Sul

Rio Branco

PERU

EXPLORE!

How many hours will it take a lorry to travel the whole length of the Trans-Amazonian Highway if its average speed is 40 km per hour, allowing for rest and fuel stops on the way?

⬅ Only 18 per cent of Brazil's total road network can be used by lorries after heavy, tropical rainfall. This section of the 5,300 km Trans-Amazonian Highway is being covered with tarmac.

N

SURINAM
•Boa Vista

Northern Perimeter Highway

•Macapá

R. Negro

R. Amazon

•Belém

Manaus

R. Tapajos

Trans-Amazonian Highway

R. Madeira

•São Luís

•Fortaleza

R. Xingu

•Teresina

•Natal

R. Tocatins

Juazeiro do Norte•

BRAZIL

Campina •Recife
Grande

R. Sao Francisco

•Cuiabá

•Salvador

Marshal Rondon Highway

✈Brasília

Cuiabá•

*South
Atlantic
Ocean*

BOLIVIA

•Goiânia

Rondonópolis•

•Belo Horizonte

Campo•
Grande

•Vitória

Rio Paraná

PARAGUAY

São Paulo ✈•Rio de Janeiro

•Curitiba

Key

━━━ Railway

──── Highway built to expand
Brazil's interior transport
network

✈ Major airport

Tropical rainforest

Deforestation

•Florianópolis

Santa Maria•
•Rio Grande

URUGUAY

| 0 | 500 miles |
| 0 | 1000 km |

The USA: Domestic airways

The USA is the fourth biggest country in the world. Its rich economy is founded on industries spread through the country, with most major cities near the east and west coasts. Two US states, Alaska and Hawaii, are separate from all the others. Transport networks are vital to link the parts of this vast country together.

There are several reasons why US travellers take over 600 million domestic flights each year. The USA has many large oilfields, so aviation fuel — and air fares — are cheap. Speed limits on US highways are lower than in many other countries and strictly controlled by the police, so road travel is slow. The sparse railway network makes many places difficult to reach by train. Nevertheless, flying does not compete well with road or rail for journeys under 500 km because of time delays on the ground, such as security checks and baggage handling.

Aircraft engines have a significant impact on the environment. They create vast amounts of greenhouse gases, notably in the upper atmosphere where their impact on global warming is greater, they cause water pollution due to run-off of chemicals from airports, and noise pollution. However, these engines are now becoming much more fuel-efficient, so they are less polluting than in the past.

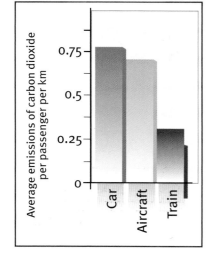

⟵ Although aircraft need a large amount of fuel per flight, the amount used per passenger is lower than if the same amount of people travelled by car.

Number of aircraft flights	29,800,000
Number of passenger journeys	1,480,000,000
Total weight of cargo carried	25,200,00 tonnes

⬆ Seven of the 20 busiest airports in the world are located in the USA. This table shows the passenger and cargo traffic in North America.

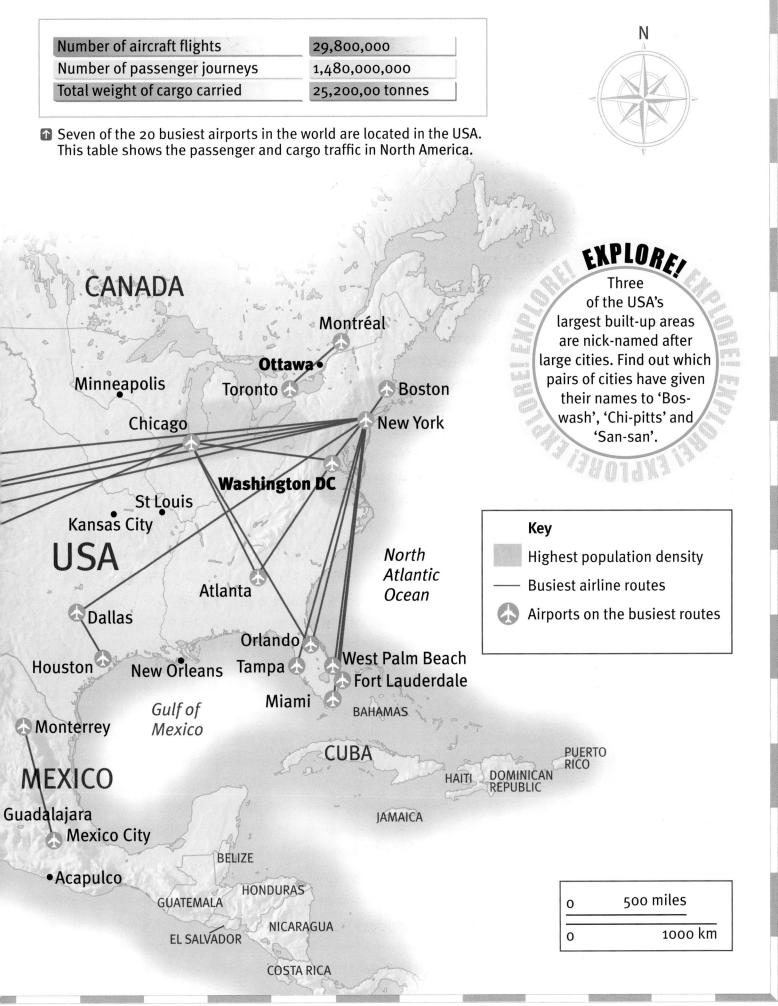

EXPLORE!

Three of the USA's largest built-up areas are nick-named after large cities. Find out which pairs of cities have given their names to 'Bos-wash', 'Chi-pitts' and 'San-san'.

Key

■ Highest population density

— Busiest airline routes

✈ Airports on the busiest routes

The world: International flights

Our world is becoming more interconnected through the export and import of goods and services, improved communication, and the migration of people. This growing contact between continents is often called globalisation.

Air travel is the quickest way to reach international destinations, which is why it has grown into a huge transport network moving both people and goods. The largest aircraft can carry over 800 people or over 200 tonnes of goods at about 900 km per hour.

Ten per cent of global goods are transported by air. Air freight has changed the speed goods move around the world and what people eat. Shoppers expect to be able to buy every kind of fresh food throughout the year, from salads to tropical fruits, because they can be transported from where they grow in chilled cargo planes to places where it is too cold or dry to grow them.

The cost of international flights is kept low for passengers because governments make jet fuel cheap in order to promote global trade, and today's planes are more fuel-efficient than in the past. But aircraft engines release more greenhouse gases per passenger than ships or trains and there is much environmental damage caused by building airports.

NORTH AMERICA

Vancouver
Las Vegas   Denver   Chicago   New York
NORTH AMERICA—ASIA
San Francisco   Dallas   NORTH AM
Los Angeles Phoenix   Atlanta
                            Houston
                        Miami

NORTH AMERICA—SOUTH A

SOUTH AMERICA

Rio de Janeiro

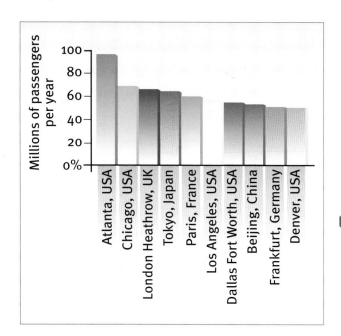

← This graph shows that the world's ten busiest airports are in the northern hemisphere. The next 20 busiest airports are also north of the Equator.

N

EUROPE

ASIA

London
Amsterdam
Frankfurt
EUROPE—ASIA

Beijing
ASIA—NORTH AMERICA

Paris

Madrid

Rome

EUROPE—SOUTH-EAST ASIA

Tokyo

EUROPE—AFRICA

Dubai

Bangkok

AFRICA

Singapore

SOUTH-EAST ASIA—AUSTRALASIA

Jakarta

AUSTRALASIA

Cape Town

Sydney

Auckland

EXPLORE!

Next time your family visits a supermarket, try to find at least one kind of food which has been grown in each continent – except Antarctica, of course!

Key

➤ The busiest air routes

➤ Other important air routes

✈ Airports on important routes

The world: Container ships

Shipping containers are large metal boxes used to carry goods by road, rail and ship since the 1950s. Before that, it took many workers a long time to load and unload shipping freight. Today, ports and docks are laid out with special cranes and transporters to rapidly load and unload containers to and from ships, trains and lorries, using fewer workers.

Ships are the cheapest way to transport heavy goods between countries. Containers are very strong and may be stacked high without goods inside being damaged. They can be used to carry anything from cars and clothes, to toys and bananas. Air freight is more suitable for goods that need to be moved fast, such as fresh shellfish or magazines, because it is more expensive per tonne carried than shipping.

Container ships do have some environmental impacts. When ports are dredged to accommodate larger container ships, this can destroy marine life. Giant container ships use lots of cheap fuel high in sulphur. This causes 50 times more air pollution per tonne carried than lorries, which use cleaner fuel. In rough seas, containers can fall off ships. Some sink, but many float just under the surface of the water, causing shipping hazards.

NORTH AMERICA

St. Lawrence Seaway

Vancouver

To Japan

San Francisco

Los Angeles

New Orleans

New Yor[k]

Pacific Ocean

Havana

Honolulu

To Japan and China

Panama Canal

SOUTH AMERI[CA]

To Australia and New Zealand

Rio de Jan[eiro]

São Pau[lo]

Santiago

Buenos Aires

To Australia and New Zealand

This ship, the *Emma Maersk*, is one of the largest container ships in the world. Fully loaded, it can carry 15,200 containers!

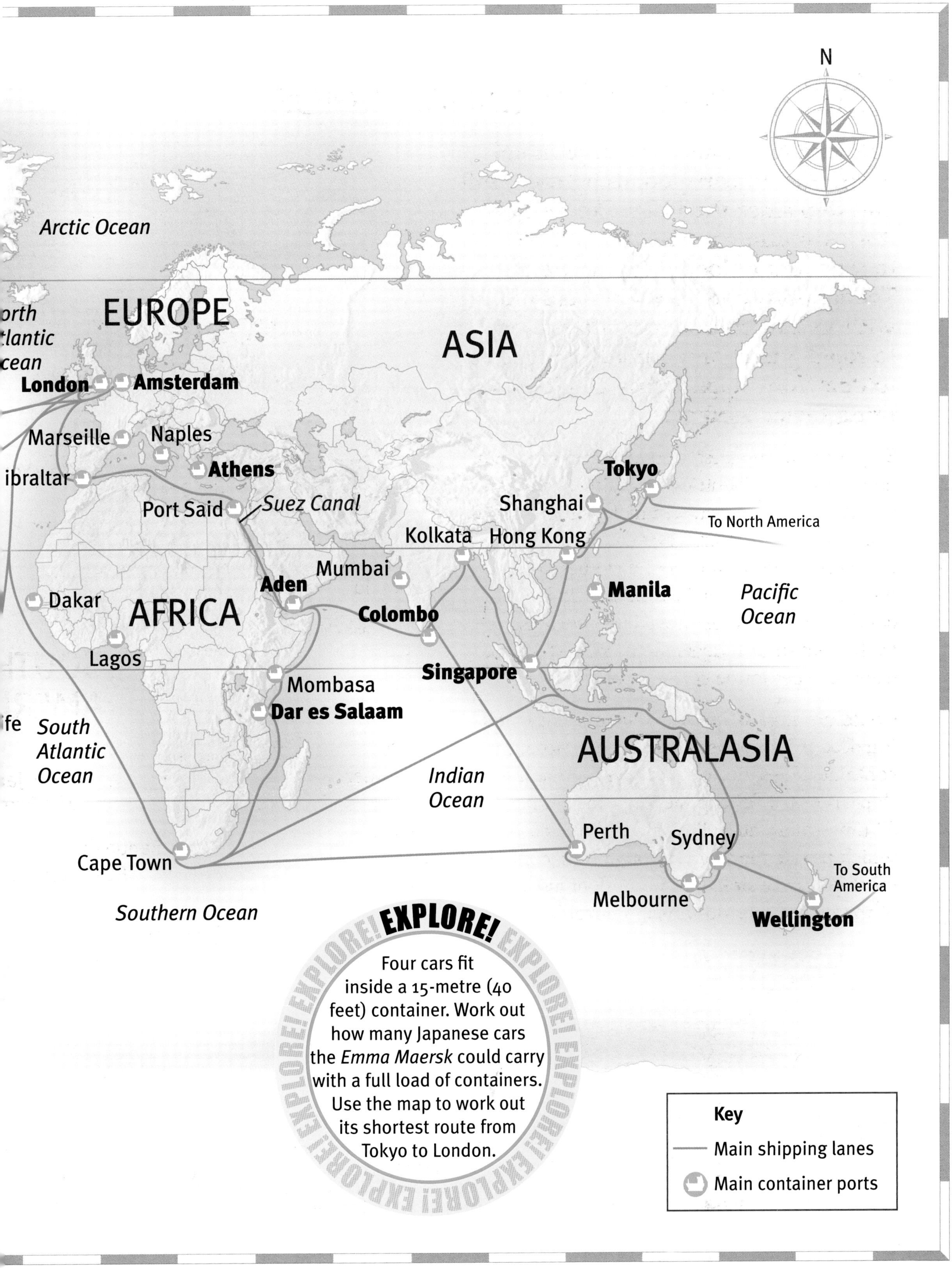
N
Arctic Ocean
EUROPE
orth
lantic
cean
London
Amsterdam
Marseille
Naples
Athens
ibraltar
Port Said
Suez Canal
ASIA
Tokyo
Shanghai
To North America
Kolkata
Hong Kong
Mumbai
Aden
Manila
Pacific Ocean
Dakar
AFRICA
Colombo
Lagos
Singapore
Mombasa
Dar es Salaam
fe
South Atlantic Ocean
AUSTRALASIA
Indian Ocean
Perth
Sydney
Cape Town
To South America
Melbourne
Wellington
Southern Ocean
Key
Main shipping lanes
Main container ports

EXPLORE!

Four cars fit inside a 15-metre (40 feet) container. Work out how many Japanese cars the *Emma Maersk* could carry with a full load of containers. Use the map to work out its shortest route from Tokyo to London.

Europe: Oil and gas pipelines

Globally, fossil fuels supply much of the energy we need to make machines work. This includes oil to power vehicles and gas to burn in power stations.

In northern Europe, oil and gas used to be imported in tankers from other continents. Then in the 1950s the Netherlands discovered large gas reserves under the North Sea. The UK, Germany, Norway and Denmark then found more gas and oil reserves through the region. These local fossil fuels cost a lot to find but do not have to be transported so far.

Pipelines are the cheapest way to transport large amounts of fuel from the reserves to land terminals, such as Sullum Voe (Shetland Islands). The fuel is then transported by ships, trains or lorries. Oil and gas pipes are usually made of steel, about 1 metre across, and can be hundreds of kilometres long. They are buried just under the sea floor and pumps keep the fuel moving.

North Sea reserves are gradually running out – they are finite, as they formed millions of years ago – so energy companies drill deeper to find more. Drilling and laying pipes damages the seafloor, and pipeline spills can pollute water. Exploration is dangerous, as people working in deep water are at risk of accidents, and fuel passing through oil and gas rigs can catch fire.

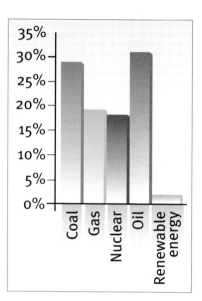

⬆ This bar graph shows that coal and gas are two of the most important sources of energy for European countries.

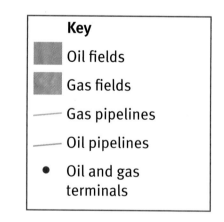

Key
- Oil fields
- Gas fields
- Gas pipelines
- Oil pipelines
- Oil and gas terminals

⬅ The Brent Delta oil rig lies in Brent field. Its oil is transported to Sullum Voe by a pipeline laid on the bottom of the sea.

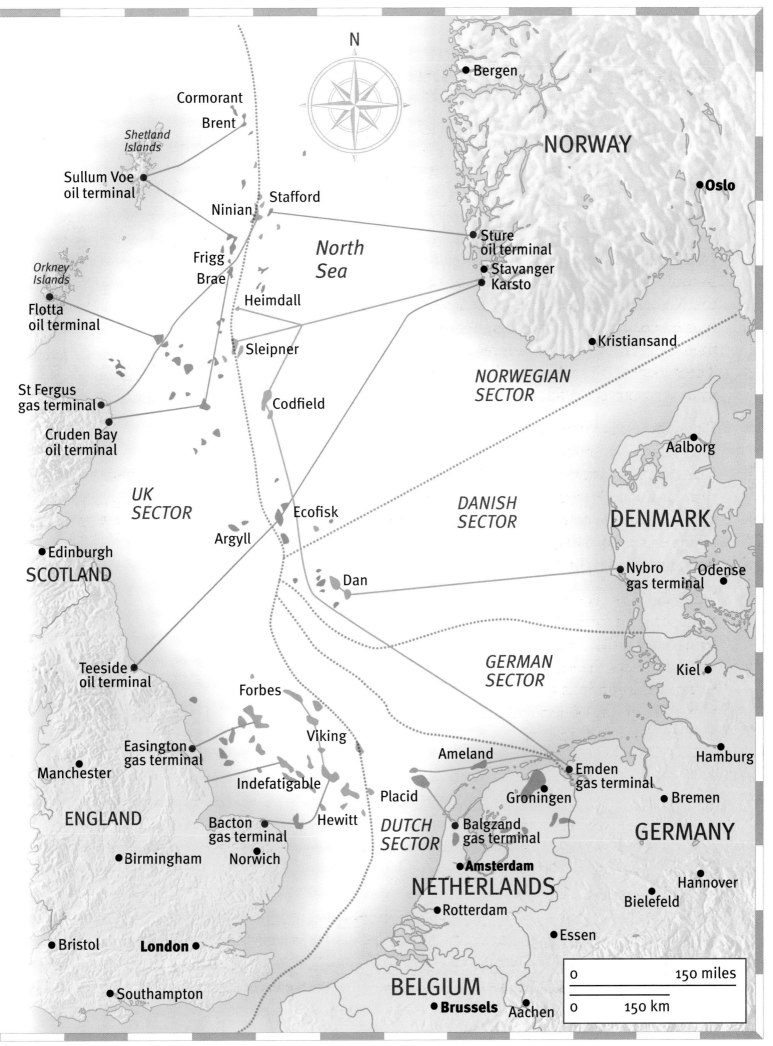

N

Cormorant
Brent
Shetland Islands
Sullum Voe oil terminal
Stafford
Ninian
Orkney Islands
Frigg
Brae
Flotta oil terminal
Heimdall
Sleipner
St Fergus gas terminal
Codfield
Cruden Bay oil terminal

North Sea

Bergen
NORWAY
Oslo
Sture oil terminal
Stavanger
Karsto
Kristiansand

NORWEGIAN SECTOR

UK SECTOR
Edinburgh
SCOTLAND
Argyll
Ecofisk

DANISH SECTOR
Aalborg
Nybro gas terminal
Odense
DENMARK
Dan

Teeside oil terminal
Forbes
Viking
GERMAN SECTOR
Kiel
Hamburg

Easington gas terminal
Manchester
Indefatigable
Hewitt
Ameland
Emden gas terminal
Bremen

ENGLAND
Placid
Groningen
GERMANY

Bacton gas terminal
Norwich
Birmingham
DUTCH SECTOR
Balgzand gas terminal
Amsterdam
NETHERLANDS
Hannover
Bielefeld

Bristol
London •
Rotterdam
Essen

Southampton
BELGIUM
Brussels
Aachen

0		150 miles
0		150 km

Western Europe:
Inland waterways

Waterways are channels used for transport. They are generally networks of rivers, sometimes straightened to make navigation of barges easier, and purpose-built canals, connected to important sea ports.

The waterways network was established in the 18th century in north-western Europe at the start of the Industrial Revolution, which originated there. This was before rail or road transport networks had been built. It was then the major way of moving heavy goods over long distances, such as coal used to power steam engines and iron ore to make steel to construct anything from ships to bridges. The map shows how canals linked with rivers and established a trans-European transport network. Large cities and industrial areas built up around waterways, because goods could be transported to and from these areas more easily.

Waterways are still used today in the region to transport coal for power stations and other heavy goods direct from ports to factories. Transporting goods by barge causes less environmental pollution than rail or road transport, and is cheap. Waterways also provide important habitats and corridors for wildlife, although traffic can also disturb wildlife and pollute water.

EXPLORE!

Investigate the geographical reasons why the waterway network did not develop in central and southern Europe and how changing transport technology might have impacted this.

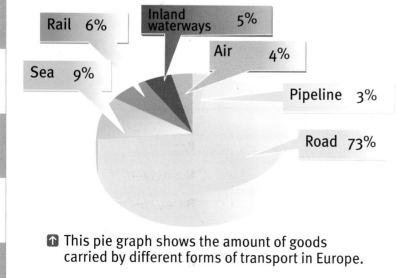

Rail 6%

Inland waterways 5%

Air 4%

Sea 9%

Pipeline 3%

Road 73%

⬆ This pie graph shows the amount of goods carried by different forms of transport in Europe.

⬆ A typical Rhine barge transporting scrap metal.

N

Kiel

Kiel Canal

Hamburg

Bremen

Hannover

Berlin

Mitteland Canal

Bielefeld

GERMANY

North Sea

NETHERLANDS

Liverpool
Hull
Manchester

ENGLAND

Norwich
Birmingham

Amsterdam

Rotterdam

London

Oostende
Antwerp
BELGIUM
Brussels
Dover
Calais
Lille
Charleroi
Aachen

Essen
Düsseldorf
Cologne

R. Rhine

Frankfurt
am Main

Nuremberg

Southampton

English Channel

LUXEMBOURG
Luxembourg

Metz

Stuttgart

Le Havre
R. Seine
R. Oise
R. Marne
Paris

Nancy
Strasbourg

R. Danube

Munich

Rennes

Orléans

R. Saone

AUSTRIA
Innsbruck
LIECHTENSTEIN

Nantes
R. Loire

FRANCE

Bern
SWITZERLAND

Zürich

Geneva

Atlantic
Ocean

Clermont-Ferrand

R. Loire

Lyon

Milan
Verona
Venice

ITALY

Bordeaux
R. Garonne

Turin

Bologna

Genoa

Florence

Toulouse

Montpellier

Nîmes

Marseille

Nice

Pisa

Canal du Midi

Mediterranean Sea

Perpignan

Key	
～～	Main rivers
━━	Barge canals
▉	Industrial areas
⬓	Major seaports

0 — 150 miles

0 — 150 km

North America: The St. Lawrence Seaway

The St. Lawrence River was first used by fur hunters and Native Americans living along its length to trade with communities around the Great Lakes. Today the widened river with a series of locks forms the St. Lawrence Seaway, which completes a 3,750 km inland waterway used by large ships to transport heavy, bulk goods to and from the interior of North America.

The main goods transported on the waterway include wheat grown in the prairies of Canada and mid-western USA, coal and iron ore from eastern reserves, and timber from Canadian forests. Some cities along the waterway have grown through using the resources. For example, Detroit is home of the US car industry. Other city ports such as Chicago and Quebec grew owing to the amount of trade through the waterway.

The St. Lawrence Seaway is so important to the economies of Canada and the USA that the countries shared the high cost of building locks in the 1960s to ease navigation. Unfortunately, the Seaway cannot be used for four months each winter as it freezes over. It has also caused environmental problems. For example, marine zebra mussels accidentally moved by ocean ships into the Great Lakes are now a nuisance because they clog pipes taking water into power plants and factories.

⬆ Cargo ships docked for the winter in Port Colborne, Canada.

EXPLORE! Find out how the St. Lawrence Seaway is monitored to prevent environmental damage to the Great Lakes.

⬅ A cargo ship transporting iron ore, passing through Soo Locks, on the border of the USA and Canada.

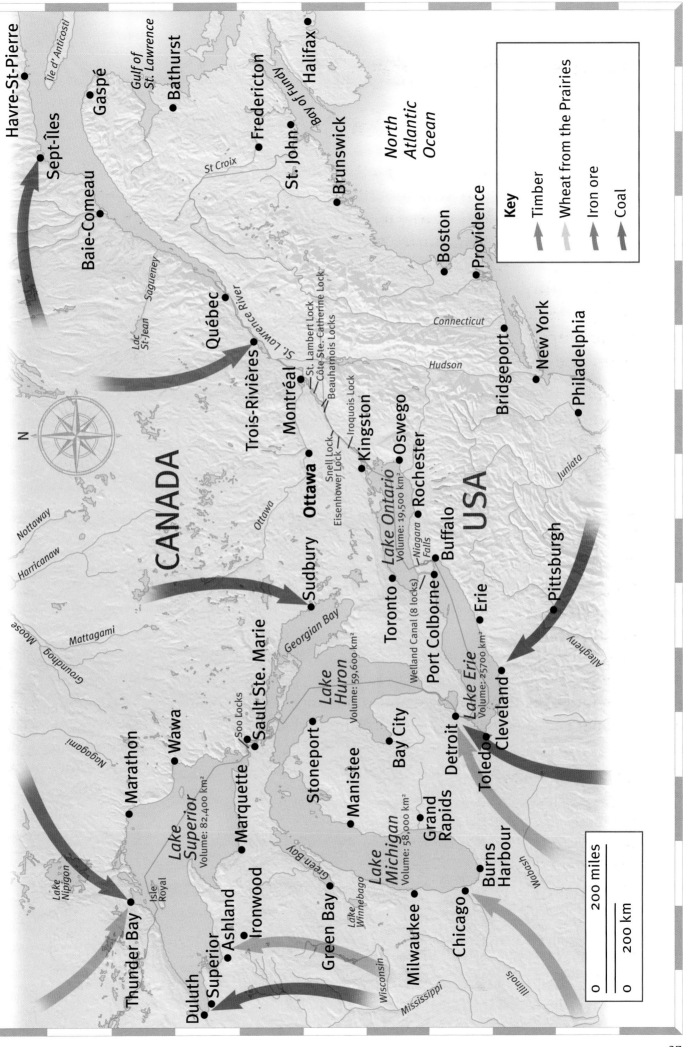

Key

Timber

Wheat from the Prairies

Iron ore

Coal

North Atlantic Ocean

Havre-St-Pierre

Île d' Anticosti

Gaspé

Gulf of St. Lawrence

Bathurst

Sept-Îles

Baie-Comeau

Fredericton

St Croix

St. John

Bay of Fundy

Halifax

Brunswick

Boston

Providence

New York

Philadelphia

Bridgeport

Québec

St. Lawrence River

Saguenay

Lac St-Jean

Connecticut

Hudson

Trois-Rivières

Montréal

St. Lambert Lock

Côte Ste.-Catherine Lock

Beauharnois Locks

Iroquois Lock

Kingston

Oswego

Rochester

N

CANADA

Ottawa

Snell Lock

Eisenhower Lock

Ottawa

Lake Ontario
Volume: 19,500 km²

USA

Juniata

Nottaway

Harricanaw

Sudbury

Niagara Falls

Buffalo

Pittsburgh

Allegheny

Georgian Bay

Toronto

Welland Canal (8 locks)

Port Colborne

Erie

Moose

Groundhog

Mattagami

Lake Huron
Volume: 59,600 km²

Lake Erie
Volume: 25700 km²

Cleveland

Soo Locks

Sault Ste. Marie

Stoneport

Bay City

Detroit

Toledo

Nagagami

Wawa

Marathon

Manistee

Burns Harbour

Lake Superior
Volume: 82,400 km²

Marquette

Ironwood

Ashland

Green Bay

Green Bay

Lake Michigan
Volume: 58,000 km²

Grand Rapids

Lake Nipigon

Isle Royal

Thunder Bay

Superior

Duluth

Lake Winnebago

Milwaukee

Chicago

Wisconsin

Mississippi

Wabash

Illinois

200 miles

0

200 km

0

West Africa: The world's longest trains

Steel is one of the world's most widely used products as it is strong, durable, and cheap. However, the problem with transporting the iron ore it is made from is that it is worth far less than the steel. Cheap transport is necessary to make steel cheap enough to sell.

Mauritania in North Africa has large reserves of iron ore far inland. There are no major waterways to transport the ore to Atlantic ports for export, because of the country's desert climate. This is why a train line was built in the 1960s by French colonists to transport iron ore as efficiently as possible. Today, iron ore makes up half of Mauritania's income from exports.

The trains running on the route are some of the biggest in the world. They are up to 3 km long with four engines and 200 carriages carrying up to 22,000 tonnes of iron ore. The railway line transports the ore from where it is mined in Zouérat to port Nouad-Hibou 700 km away. It is exported across the world to countries including China and India. Passengers use the train, mostly sitting on the ore. Dust from the ore covers the people and their luggage.

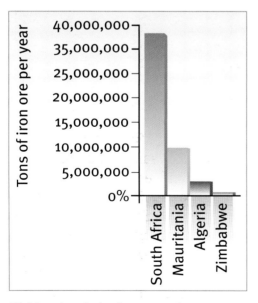

⬆ Mauritania is the second most important source of iron ore in Africa after South Africa.

⬆ Passengers can travel free, but have to sit in the open, on top of the iron ore in the wagons. A passenger carriage has been added to some trains, but people have to pay to use it.

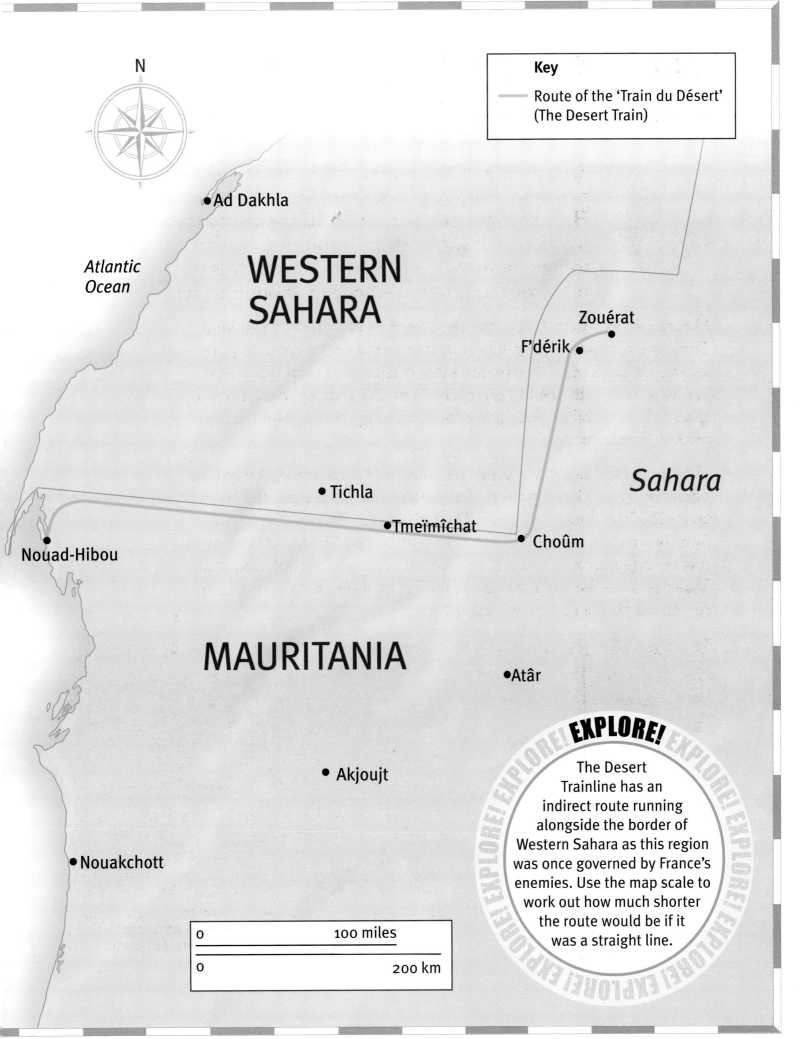

N

Key
— Route of the 'Train du Désert' (The Desert Train)

Atlantic Ocean

●Ad Dakhla

WESTERN SAHARA

Sahara

Zouérat
●
F'dérik ●

● Tichla

●Tmeïmîchat
● Choûm

Nouad-Hibou
●

MAURITANIA

●Atâr

EXPLORE!

The Desert Trainline has an indirect route running alongside the border of Western Sahara as this region was once governed by France's enemies. Use the map scale to work out how much shorter the route would be if it was a straight line.

● Akjoujt

●Nouakchott

0	100 miles
0	200 km

Now test yourself!

These questions will help you to revisit some of the information in this book. To answer the questions, you will need to use the contents on page 2 and the index on page 32, as well as the relevant pages on each topic.

1 Use the contents list on page 2 to find which pages show a map of:

(a) Africa's longest goods train.

(b) the world's busiest shipping routes.

(c) the busiest airports in Britain and Asia.

2 Use the index on page 32 to find the pages that will tell you:

(a) which European sea supplies Britain with oil as well as natural gas.

(b) how ships can sail inland across parts of North America.

(c) whether tourists can travel by train to reach the centre of the Amazon rainforest in Brazil.

3 Use the glossary on page 31 to complete a copy of this table:

Key word	Meaning of this word
Domestic route	
	People moving somewhere else to live and work
Population	

4 Use pages 10–11 to name the Australian tourist trains that will let you:

(a) travel on this continent's longest railway journey.

(b) visit the Aborigines' most sacred rock.

5 Using pages 12–13, write down which Italian motorways you would use to travel from Palermo to Genoa by the shortest possible route.

6 Use pages 24–25 to find out which of these waterway journeys can be completed by using only a canal; only a river; both a canal and a river:

(a) Nantes to Orleans.

(b) Paris to Strasbourg.

(c) Berlin to Hanover.

9 Use page 27 to put the Great Lakes in size order, starting with the largest lake.

10 Use pages 16–19 to name the busiest domestic and international airport on the Pacific coast of the USA.

11 (a) Which ship canal is shown in this map?

(b) Which major port is shown in this map?

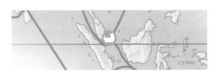

Glossary

accessible easy to get to.

commuter a person who travels to work every day.

container a huge steel box used to carry goods by road, rail and sea.

deforestation the process of clearing away trees from an area.

domestic route a route between places in the same country.

economic development the way a country and its people increase their income.

exports goods sent out of a country.

globalisation the process by which regions have become connected through a world-wide (global) network of communication, transportation, and trade.

greenhouse effect the warming effect caused by certain gases in the atmosphere that trap the heat rising from the Earth's surface.

greenhouse gas a gas in the atmosphere that traps the Sun's heat.

imports goods brought into a country.

international route a route between places in different countries.

migration people moving somewhere else to live and work.

pollution any change that makes the world a less healthy or pleasant place in which to live.

population the total number of people living in a place.

topological map a simple plan which makes a transport network much easier to understand.

tourist someone who travels and stays in other places for pleasure.

transport/transportation the movement of people and goods between places.

trade the movement of imports and exports between countries.

waterway a canal or river which is wide enough for cargo-carrying barges to use.

Index

Published in paperback in 2014 by Wayland
Copyright © Wayland 2014

Wayland
Hachette Children's Books
338 Euston Road
London NW1 3BH

Wayland Australia
Level 17/207
Kent Street
Sydney, NSW 2000

All rights reserved.

Editor: Julia Adams
Designer: Rob Walster, Big Blu Design
Cover design: Wayland
Map art: Martin Sanders
Illustrations: Andy Stagg
Picture research: Kathy Lockley/Julia Adams

The website addresses (URLs) included in this book were valid at the time of going to press. However, it is possible that contents or addresses may have changed since the publication of this book No responsibility for any such changes can be accepted by either the author or the Publisher.

British Library Cataloguing in Publication Data
Gillett, Jack.
  Maps of the environmental world.
  Transport networks.
  1. Transportation--Environmental aspects--Juvenile literature. 2. Transportation--Environmental aspects--Maps for children.
  I. Title II. Gillett, Meg.
  388-dc22

ISBN 978 0 7502 8275 8
Printed in Malaysia
10 9 8 7 6 5 4 3 2 1

Wayland is a division of Hachette Children's Books, an Hachette UK company.
www.hachette.co.uk

Picture acknowledgements:
All photography: Shutterstock, execpt: p. 6 Wikipedia; p. 10 Great Southern Rail, Australia; p. 20 Vincent Jannink/epa/Corbis; p. 22 Brian Jobson/Alamy; p. 28 dbimages/Alamy